MW00803533

The Spirit Man In Her

May you be blessed
by the message
contained in this
book. To God be all
the Glory.

Elder Cheryl Chaline

The Spirit Man In Her

Cheryl E. Chavis

Copyright © 2009 by Cheryl E. Chavis.

ISBN: Softcover   978-1-4363-8474-2

All rights reserved. No part of this book may be reproduced or transmitted in any form or by any means, electronic or mechanical, including photocopying, recording, or by any information storage and retrieval system, without permission in writing from the copyright owner.

All scripture quotations are taken from The Holy Bible.

King James Version   Used by Permission

Broadman & Holman Publishers Nashville, Tennessee

This book was printed in the United States of America.

To order additional copies of this book, contact:
Xlibris Corporation
1-888-795-4274
www.Xlibris.com
Orders@Xlibris.com
53732

This Book Is Dedicated

First and Foremost to my Lord and Saviour Jesus Chirst

&

To my Pastor (the late) Bishop M. Alleyne
House of the Lord Jesus Christ
Apostolic Faith, Inc.
Boston, MA

&

To my mother Co-Pastor Elizabeth Carrick
Resurrection Community Baptist Church
Boston, MA

Special Acknowledgements to the Following People

Whose Major Contributions Inspired Me To Write What Thus
Sayest The Lord.

My Loving husband and Pastor Elder Fredrick D. Chavis,
has always been my biggest fan and supporter.

My Loving son Fredrick I. Chavis
became my personal assistant and computer teacher.

My husband's uncle Elder Johnjas Hedrick Sr.
taught the series "Will the Real Preacher Stand Up"
on our church radio broadcast.

TABLE OF CONTENTS

PREFACE

This book was written for God's Glory to be manifested in his people.

After all we were created to worship and praise him in season and out of season.

It is time for those in captivity to be set free from the bounds of the enemy.

From the time I was born my destiny has always involved helping others. If this

book helps one person then it has served its purpose. However it is my hope that

it will help many to understand what we were created for. Thank you Jesus you

are the author, and finisher, of our faith.

Man of God and Woman of God behold the word of the Lord Jesus Christ.

Walk in the destiny of truth and be not deceived.

Introduction

Does Jesus call women to preach his gospel? Yes or no. This is a question for the history books. Man verses woman has been a debate for centuries.

However in the word of God somebody is right and somebody is wrong. There is only one book with the answer to this heavily debated topic. The one and only true book of life is "The Holy Bible".

There is only one interpretation or one interpreter. The question is whose report will you believe? (Isaiah 53:1) "Who hath believed our report? and to whom is the arm of the Lord revealed?"

Women have managed to come out of the home and infiltrate almost every profession known to man. We have endured, adopted and over came every obstacle in our midst. Why do I say infiltrate because there are still people today who believe a woman's place is in, the home. I wonder if they heard the expression "home is where the heart is".

In the King James Version of the Holy Bible it is written in (Jeremiah 1:5) "Before I formed thee in the belly I knew thee; and before thou camest forth out of the womb I sanctified thee, and I ordained thee a prophet unto the nations."

There is only one who knows you in your mother's womb and he is Lord of Lord's and King of Kings. He alone is God.

The first ordination is by God himself. He equips you and sends you out to the nations. A prophet is a preacher. We speak, teach and pray by the inspiration of the Holy Spirit. We did not ask to be preachers. We were chosen and called from our mothers' wombs. Male and female here we are, strong and weak, near and far.

Chapter 1

Husband and Wife

Before one can understand the roles of husband and wife they must first understand the roles of male and female. The order of the church is directly related to the husband and wife. Let us look at the following scripture in the New Testament.

(1st Corithians 14:34) "Let your women keep silence in the churches: for it is not permitted unto them to speak; but they are commanded to be under obedience, as also saith the law."

This is the number one scripture that men have been using as the basis that women are not allowed to preach. The scripture above that one is conveniently overlooked and it states as follows: (1st Corithians 14:33) "For God is not the author of confusion, but of peace, as in all churches of the saints."

You cannot understand preaching unless you have been taught. Please study the Bible and know it for yourself. It said it clearly in (2nd Timothy 2:15) "Study to shew thyself approved unto God, a workman that needeth not to be ashamed, rightly dividing the word of truth."

Clearly this was not the confusion that was going on in the church. The confusion was women were bringing in personal matters of the home. Something you are not supposed to do; back then or even today. When it comes to husband and wife one should never bring their home problems into the church for an open discussion. That's what causes confusion with God's people. Here is an example, a woman states to another "my husband does this . . ." Then the other woman quite naturally responds in agreement or disagreement of what is going on in the other woman's household. Other women listening become drawn into the conversation.

Next the man gets a whole of what has transpired and before you know it two groups have formed. The men versus the women, battle of the sexes in full force.

It does not take a genius to figure out the women will side with each other against the men. Total chaos and turmoil pursue until the peace of God intervenes.

The scripture in 1st Corithians 14:34 had nothing to do with the preaching of the gospel. It is a domestic scripture. Any time you see husband and wife those are domestic scriptures that pertain to the home. Look at (1st Corithians 7:14) "For the unbelieving husband is sanctified by the wife, and the unbelieving wife is sanctified by the husband: else were your children unclean; but now are they holy." This is why both husband and wife must speak edifying words. Husband and wife are symbolizing how the church should be; one in the spirit and one in the flesh. (Genesis 2:24) "Therefore shall a man leave his father and his mother, and shall cleave unto his wife: and they shall be one flesh." According to the word in Matthew 9:15 he is our bridegroom and we are married to him it states as follows: "And Jesus said unto them, Can the children of the bridechamber mourn, as long as the bridegroom is with them? but the days will come, when the bridegroom shall be taken from them, and then shall they fast."

Jesus is the only one who was taken from us in the flesh but yet is with us in the spirit.

If a woman's husband is not saved he can be won over by her conversations and actions. The same can be said vice or versa. (1st Corinthians 7:16) "For what knowest thou, O wife, whether thou shalt save thy husband? or how knowest thou, O man, whether thou shalt save thy wife?"

Do not mix home with the spirit. Watch your conversation when you come to the church. As a matter of fact be mindful of what you say to and around others. Why, because there is one who hears all conversations and he will do the judging.

When you come to the church there should only be one thing on your mind and that is salvation. In other words there should not be any personal discussions of the home. Especially television shows and yes that includes soap operas. Yes I know church folks watch soap operas. I use to be one until I got delivered by the word of God.

Your only objective should be praising and lifting up the name of Jesus for the healing and deliverance of your soul. Any other objective will result in destruction. (1st Timothy 4:1) "Now the spirit speaketh expressly, that in the latter times some shall depart from the faith, giving heed to seducing spirits, and doctrines of devils."

You know Paul also said in (1st Corinthians 14:28) "But if there be no interpreter, let him keep silence in the church; and let him speak to himself, and to God."

That scripture was written first but yet it is overlooked. Do you know why because of lack of understanding of the word of God. The same word he said to me is the same word he said to you. God is no respecter of persons.

Adam was first then came Eve. They had nothing to do with the preaching of the gospel. After all they were husband and wife. Wives must submit themselves to their husbands in the home and in the church. However God is the head of both of them in all things.

Chapter 2

Male and Female

When one does not study the word they become like the word said in the book of (Malachi 2:8) "But ye are departed out of the way; ye have caused many to stumble at the law; ye have corrupted the covenant of Levi, saith the Lord of hosts."

His word holds forth true today as it did back then. Decade after decade women have been fighting for equal rights. Today we will make a stand and we will be heard.

The devil has launched an attack against the word of God. When the men are talking about women cannot preach or teach in the churches or stand in the pulpits, they are being used by the devil.

It is not against the women that this evil has been aimed at. The hidden target is the word of God. Why? Because Jesus is the one who called women to preach.

(I John 4:6) said "We are of God: He that knoweth God heareth us; he that is not of God heareth not us. Hereby know we the spirit of truth, and the spirit of error."

The devil is laughing at how easily he can deceive us using our own devices. One word out of context can make a nation stumble. But thank God for those who are studying the word by the master himself our Lord Jesus. (Galatians 3:27) "For as many of you as have been baptized into Christ have put on Christ." Search your heart and ask yourself have you truly been baptized into Christ. (Galatians 3:28) "There is neither Jew nor Greek, there is neither bond nor free, there is neither male nor female: for ye are all one in Christ Jesus."

As you can see in the word before you, we are all one in Christ Jesus. There is no male or female salvation. Jesus has no respect of persons. Why do you practice what your father does not? If you are not one with Jesus Christ our Lord then ye are none of his. You will be as the word said in (Ezekiel 7:15) "The Sword is without, and the pestilence and the famine within: he that is in the field shall die with the sword; and he that is in the city, famine and pestilence shall devour him." The sword is symbolic as the word. It must be on the inside in order to stop sin and starvation of the spirit man inside of you. Are you feeding your spirit the right food?

Jesus yields to man as head of household. When one is down on their knees praying for supplication, trying to get what they have need of from the Lord, submission takes place. There is submission in the church to man and the Lord. Both of us must submit ourselves to the Lord. Your submission to God is greater than to man. Look at (1st Timothy 2:11) "Let the woman learn in silence with all subjection." This is a domestic scripture for husband and wife. (Luke 4:18)" The spirit of the Lord is upon me, because he hath anointed me to preach the gospel to the poor; he hath sent me to heal the brokenhearted, to preach deliverance to the captives, and recovering of sight to the blind, to set at liberty them that are bruised, (Luke 4:19) "To preach the acceptable year of the Lord." Again I say Jesus is the head of the church not man.

Chapter 3

Who Is The Preacher?

The preacher is a man or woman hired by Jesus. We are hired by the qualifications that Jesus has put in us, and he is the boss.

Do you know that every man that has spoken against the women preaching and teaching is wrong. They have yet to learn what thou meanest in (1st Timothy 2:12) "But I suffer not a woman to teach, nor to usurp authority over the man, but to be in silence." They will have to give an account of their actions to the Lord Jesus for what they have spoken. Did he not say in (Matthew 18:6) "But whoso shall offend one of these little ones which believe in me, it were better for him that a millstone were hanged about his neck, and that he were drowned in the depth of the sea." Every one of us is God's little ones when we humble ourselves and seek him. Read the verse in (Matthew 18:7) "Woe unto the world because of offenses! for it must needs be that offences come; but woe to that man by whom the offence commeth!"

In the word of God it said my sheep know my voice and a stranger they will not follow. It does not say my sheep know my flesh. We need to stop looking at the outward appearance. One cannot determine God's voice by looking upon a person's flesh. It is not the flesh that's speaking. (2nd Corinthians 4:5) "For we preach not ourselves, but Christ Jesus the Lord; and ourselves your servants for Jesus' sake."

Looking at the condition that the world is in right now, so many people have not been hired by Jesus. This is what it means to be preaching without the Holy Ghost. Hurricanes, earthquakes so much flooding and droughts, one would ascertain that we are in trouble. People are writing down sermons trying to do this ministry and work without Jesus. As long as you put Jesus first there is nothing wrong with writing sermons. This work cannot be done without him. You must step aside and let him do the work in you. If you are preaching without Jesus you are a lying preacher. The same word goes if prophesying without the Lord Jesus; it all equals a lying prophet.

Here's an example, a preacher gives a message on healing and there is a person present who has no faith. You need faith to be healed. (Hebrews 11:6) "But without faith it is impossible to please him: for he that cometh to God must believe that he is, and that he is a rewarder of them that diligently seek him."

Most of all you need to know who the healer is. (Exodus 15:26) "And said, If thou wilt diligently hearken to the voice of the Lord thy God, and wilt do that which is right in his sight, and wilt give ear to his commandments, and keep all his statutes, I will put none of these diseases upon thee, which I have brought upon the Egyptians: for I am the Lord that healeth thee."

The Lord always discerns the needs of all his people present in the congregation whether its 10 or 5,000. How many can you discern? What happens when there is a language barrier? You cannot speak every language, but the Lord Jesus Christ who made us can do all things. He gave some the gift of diversities of tongues so that he can use us to speak to his people in their own language. Our God is intelligent and covers all the bases. There is no task too hard for him and no obstacle that he cannot move.

You certainly cannot heal anyone without Jesus. Yes people have tried to, only they ended up needing somebody to lay hands on them. The devil knows who the preacher is. Look what he did to the men who tried to bind him. He sent them running out of the house naked. You can read it for yourself in the book of (Acts 19:13-20). That's why Jesus tells us to focus on him, and not on others, which brings us back to where we started. (2nd Corinthians 4:5) "For we preach not ourselves, but Christ Jesus the Lord; and ourselves your servants for Jesus' sake." As one can see, we are not the ones doing the preaching, neither can we presume to tell others they are not; flesh and blood has nothing to do with the preaching of the gospel. Its not about us any how, it's all about Jesus.

Jesus called all of us unto him for salvation that he might cleanse our bodies, minds, and souls. He freely gives us the gift of the Holy Ghost. The Holy Ghost is his spirit dwelling on the inside and working on the outside. In other words the Holy Ghost is the preacher not the woman or the man.

I have a word to give unto those who speak false messages. You cannot silence the spirit that is in them; but you can silence the women, if they surrender to this nonsense. Women of God hear ye now what thus sayest the Lord. "Speak what I put in thine mouth and be not afraid of their faces for I am with thee."

Our Lord Jesus will teach, preach and do anything he desires, including healing and prophesying. (1st Corinthians 14:35) "And if they will learn any thing, let them ask their husbands at home: for it is a shame for women to speak in the church." You will learn at home from the head of household which usually is the man. This verse has nothing to do with the church. Jesus is the head of the church. (Ephesians 2:20-22)

"And are built upon the foundation of the apostles and prophets, Jesus Christ himself being the chief corner stone; In whom all the building fitly framed together growth unto an holy temple in the Lord: In whom ye also are builded together for an habitation of God through the spirit." You cannot build a natural building without a foundation. The same can be said about the spirit. Our bodies are the buildings that grow by the teachings of the Holy Spirit. As the word increases in us the spirit man transforms our mind, body, and soul into a temple; a holy habitation in which our Lord lives in and has his being in us. If one is to learn anything how can they hear without a preacher? The preaching of the gospel comes from the spirit. It is a wonderful gift of the spirit to be able to preach the gospel to his people.

Again I just want to emphasize these particular verses in (1st Timothy 2:11-15).

Verse 11 "Let the woman learn in silence with all subjection."

Verse 12 "But I suffer not a woman to teach, nor to usurp authority over the man, but to be in silence."

Verse 13 "For Adam was first formed, then Eve."

Verse 14 "And Adam was not deceived, but the woman being deceived was in the transgression."

Verse 15 "Notwithstanding she shall be saved in childbearing, if they continue in faith and charity and holiness with sobriety."

Once again these scriptures pertain to the flesh; showing forth husbands and wives in their individual roles in life. Nobody can learn anything if all of us are talking at the same time. We all know who was 1st and who was 2nd; some of us are reminded of that every where we go.

The sad fact is these men and women are not just turning away women out of their pulpits and churches, but they are turning away Jesus the one who they profess daily. Come with me in your Bible to I John the fourth chapter and look at the first four verses. Verse one "Beloved, believe not every spirit, but try the spirits whether they are of God: because many false prophets are gone out into the world." Listen there is a difference between flesh speaking and spirit speaking. What do you hear? Verse two "Hereby know ye the Spirit of God: Every spirit that confesseth that Jesus Christ is come in the flesh is of God:" Are the words that this person is speaking coming from the Bible? Is there any truth in what they are saying? These are the two most important questions one should be asking themselves whenever a person is preaching the gospel. Their outward appearance does not matter it's what is on the inside manifesting on the outside. Verse three "And every spirit that confesseth not that Jesus Christ is come in the flesh is not of God: and this is that spirit of antichrist, whereof ye have heard that it should come; and even now already is it in the world." I'm just letting the spirit talk through the word. If there is no truth to what they are speaking they are not of God. It does not matter whether they are male or female. Verse four "Ye are of God, little children, and overcome them: because greater is he that is in you, than he that is in the world." These scriptures are to live for. It is by his spirit that these women including myself are preaching and teaching the gospel of Jesus Christ. He gave the authority to us along with the power to bring the messages forth to his people.

Our destiny and calling are from our mothers' wombs. We cannot change our destiny or our calling to suit others. The word said so in the book of Jeremiah chapter one verse five. There are lists of things that can be changed but these two are not part of that list. (1st Peter 3:1) "Likewise, ye wives, be in subjection to your own husbands; that, if any obey not the word, they also may without the word be won by the conversation of the wives; (1st Peter 3:2) "While they behold your chaste conversation coupled with fear." Words can make or break you. When your conversation is holy it is easy to win over a soul. That goes for male or female, rich, or poor. You must speak the things that be of God, who is our Lord and Saviour Jesus Christ. All the apostles were on one accord and were preaching the same message; the gospel of our Lord Jesus Christ which is and was and is now to come.

Chapter 4

Do you know who you belong to?

The majority of our errors are made because we do not know who we are spiritually and naturally. The only way you are going to know who you are is to know first who you belong to. Yes everyone belongs to somebody and that somebody is The Lord of Glory.

The apostles could speak on one accord because they knew who they belonged to. Some of us do not know who God is and are out there misleading his people. (Ephesians 4:18) "Having the understanding darkened, being alienated from the life of God through the ignorance that is in them, because of the blindness of their heart:" (Ephesians 4:19) "Who being past feeling have given themselves over unto lasciviousness, to work all uncleanness with greediness." (Ephesians 4:20-21) "But ye have not so learned Christ; If so be that ye have heard him, and have been taught by him, as the truth is in Jesus:"

That which ye have just read is because you do not know who you belong unto. When you know who you belong to, then can you hear from heaven. You will not be like a ship so easily rocked from side to side. Please go get your Bible and read these scriptures: (Philippians 2:10-11) "That at the name of Jesus every knee should bow, of things in heaven, and things in earth, and things under the earth; And that every tongue should confess that Jesus Christ is Lord, to the glory of God the father." The same word is in the Old Testament please read Isaiah 44:24. Yes, God has a name just like you and me, and his name is Jesus. Now remember the Ten Commandments in the book of Exodus the 20th chapter verses 1through 6. He is not giving his glory to any man. Please read his word in Philippians 2:1-9. I am just showing the Old and the New Testament with the same message. You must get knowledge with understanding, that is what equals wisdom. (Proverbs 4:7) "Wisdom is the principal thing; therefore get wisdom: and with all thy getting get understanding." God's wisdom surpasses all of our understanding and knowledge.

It all comes down to one thing, who are you spending time with? More importantly who is occupying all of your time? I invite you to spend some time with the Lord Jesus Christ. Try doing this everyday on a daily basis. Every chance you can spend some time with the Lord do it. Never ever pass up an opportunity to spend time with Jesus.

There's a song that saids "Have you tried Jesus he's all right." I can guarantee you he's more than all right. I am sure many others can attest to that fact because we all are living testimonies.

Now getting back to the mystery of who do you belong to requires us to look back in Exodus the 20th chapter and read verse one and two. He is a jealous God and he told us from the beginning "I am." Did he not tell Moses "I am has sent you."

The same God that is in Genesis that said "Let there be light" is the same God that told Lazarus to "come forth from the grave." He that was dead four days surely came alive. Read it for yourself in St. John 11:43. No man can make the dead come back alive again, only God. And yes God has a name just like you and me. His name is Jesus the Lord of Glory. This same God spoke in Joel 2:28 and 29. I am not able to put all the scriptures pertaining to this point in this book. You must believe in Jesus Christ. The mind of Christ must be in you. Please look at (Galatians 3:27) "For as many of you as have been baptized into Christ have put on Christ."

You will recognize the spirit of God preaching and teaching in that woman. What's on the outside will not matter only the word coming forth from the inside.

Again I ask the most important question in your life; who do you belong to?

We go through rough times and do not know where to turn. It's hard to know whom to go to in times like these. We all do not go through the same things but we battle the same devil. He's the one whispering in our ear to give up and do not fight. Any lie he can think of to deceive and distract you he will whisper in your ear. It is time to pull down all the strong holds. I wanted to let you know that Jesus is "I am" and "I am "is our God.

(Revelation 22:12) "And, behold, I come quickly; and my reward is with me, to give every man according as his work shall be." There shall be none before him, and none after him. There is only one name that can heal, save, and deliver us. Jesus is the only one who can forgive you of all your sins.

The devil's job is to destroy you. What better way to destroy you than to stop you from knowing who you belong to. (2nd Corinthians 4:3) "But if our gospel be hid, it is hid to them that are lost:" What did the word say in the 5th verse. (2nd Corinthians 4:5) "For we preach not ourselves, but Christ Jesus the Lord; and ourselves your servants for Jesus' sake."

God does not reveal himself to an unbeliever. If you don't believe in God and accept him then you remain in darkness. As long as you are in darkness you don't know who you belong to. That's the way the devil wants you to be. You cannot serve who you do not know. Ask your self these three questions. Who created all things? Who died on the cross for all our sins? Who is the power inside of you? The answer to all 3 questions is Jesus Christ our Lord and Saviour. He is the invisible God that we cannot see with our natural eyes, but know without a shadow of a doubt that he is present in the midst of us.

(Titus 2:11) "For the grace of God that bringeth salvation hath appeared to all men,"

(Titus 2:12) "Teaching us that, denying ungodliness and worldly lusts, we should live soberly, righteously, and godly, in this present world;"

(Titus 2:13) "Looking for that blessed hope, and the glorious appearing of the great God and our Saviour Jesus Christ."

(Titus 2:14) "Who gave himself for us, that he might redeem us from all iniquity, and purify unto himself a peculiar people, zealous of good works."

Seek him out for yourself. Do not let any man or woman stop you from doing God's will in the name of Jesus. What have you got to lose? Please think on the matter very carefully because time is running out.

Chapter 5

Divine Assignment

The devil's job is to seek and to destroy. (1st Peter 5:8) "Be sober, be vigilant; because your adversary the devil, as a roaring lion, walketh about, seeking whom he may devour:" The devil makes it his business to know who you are, especially those who are a threat to him. Have you ever wondered who you are in Christ? I know I have on more than one occasion. My God has never left me alone.

Your destiny must be revealed to you in order to bring you out of darkness. (Isaiah 42:16) "And I bring the blind by a way that they knew not; I will lead them in paths that they have not known: I will make darkness light before them, and crooked things straight. These things will I do unto them, and not forsake them."

The devil does not care whether you are a male or a female. In fact he does not care about your color, creed or nationality. He is a bad spirit and we want no part of him in or around us.

The devil has you right where he wants you; clueless to your destiny. (Psalms 18:28) "For thou wilt light my candle: the Lord my God will enlighten my darkness."

Yes, I am still talking about women in ministry. There are still a lot of us who do not know our assignment. You have a natural and a spiritual assignment. For some people their natural and spiritual assignments are the same. There are other people who have different ones.

One thing is for sure, every one of us has a divine assignment that impacts others as well as ourselves. Do you know your assignment woman of God? This is how the devil cuts you off before you even get started. We cannot afford to slack off on our jobs; once we accept Jesus Christ as our Lord and Saviour.

Three things happen when we accept Jesus as our Lord and Saviour. The first is repentance, giving up our old ways. Secondly is obedience and third is belief. We must believe that he is the almighty God and besides him there is no other. (John 8:24) "I said therefore unto you, that ye shall die in your sins: for if ye believe not that I am he, ye shall die in your sins."

Your divine assignment is the key to your destiny. There is only one person who can tell your destiny. He is the only one who knows your heart, body, mind and soul.

Time is running out for all those playing church. It is certainly running out for all those making themselves Gods' over his people.(1st Corinthians 14:27) "If any man speak in an unknown tongue, let it be by two, or at the most by three, and that by course; and let one interpret." (1st Corinthians 14:28) "But if there be no interpreter, let him keep silence in the church; and let him speak to himself, and to God." Paul also said "let him keep silent." This is of course one of the many scriptures that men over look. In other words man of God if you are not edifying the saints in the church you need to be quiet.

You see we must encourage one another daily. The strong help the weak to achieve their destiny and fulfill their divine assignment.

Men and women are helpers to one another in every environment. Where would some of us be without the women helping?

Too many churches have made their pulpits an acting debut. The church is not a play place for showing off your talents. Your talents are a very important part of your destiny that is revealed by Jesus. The devil does what he can to keep your destiny hidden by his crafty devices. For example some preachers like to speak in Hebrew and give their own interpretation. There are few people who understand this language completely, especially as a second language. These same preachers are trying to give their own interpretation and definition to the people of God. The people have no way to verify whether it is right or wrong unless they speak the language.

That's why God said let him keep silent. Paul was speaking to both the man and the woman. We need to listen in the spirit and see in the spirit. That way we are less likely to speak from the flesh point of view. We will not look at the outward appearance but listen to the words coming forth out of the vessel of the Lord. Let us remember the word. We all learn from Jesus who is our God. (Ephesians 4:11-13) "And he gave some, apostles; and some, prophets; and some, evangelists; and some, pastors and teachers;" Verse 12: "For the perfecting of the saints, for the work of the ministry, for the edifying of the body of Christ:" Verse 13: "Till we all come in the unity of the faith, and of the knowledge of the Son of God, unto a perfect man, unto the measure of the stature of the fullness of Christ:" The man himself has to submit to the Holy Ghost. There is no separation of the two. Both male and female must submit themselves unto the Lord Jesus.

The only submission that will unlock your divine assignment is unto the Lord Jesus. (Galatians 3:28) "There is neither Jew nor Greek, there is neither bond nor free, there is neither male nor female: for ye are all one in Christ Jesus." (Galatians 3:29) "And if ye be Christ's, then are ye Abrahams's seed, and heirs according to the promise."

Divine assignment has no specific sex. Jesus is saying unto us "I am neither male nor female. What I do through one I will do through another. I am no respecter of persons. I will work through a woman just as well as a man." (1st Corinthians 11:3) "But I would have you know, that the head of every man is Christ; and the head of the woman is the man; and the head of Christ is God." Jesus is the Holy Ghost and the preacher. He came down on earth to preach and to teach and is still doing it. (Ephesians 4:8) "Wherefore he saith, When he ascended up on high, he led captivity captive, and gave gifts unto men."

Does this mean women don't have gifts? No, it does not; please look at the previous verse. (Ephesians 4:7) "But unto every one of us is given grace according to the measure of the gift of Christ." His grace comes with every gift that is given to men and women. (Ephesians 4:9) "(Now that he ascended, what is it but that he also descended first into the lower parts of the earth?" I'm just showing you the same one who went up is the same one who came down. Our Lord Jesus Christ is the giver of gifts to all mankind.

Your gifts unlock your assignments in one way or another. Gifts are without repentance but one cannot operate them in the fullness until they come to Jesus. You must receive the power on the inside to manifest it on the outside. The power on the inside is the Holy Ghost the spirit of truth. (Acts19:13) "Then certain of the vagabond Jews, exorcists, took upon them to call over them which had evil spirits the name of the Lord Jesus, saying, We adjure you by Jesus whom Paul preacheth." You cannot use the name without the power. They did not know him but were trying to use his name. (Acts 19:14) "And there were seven sons of one Sceva, a Jew, and chief of the priests, which did so." (Acts 19:15) "And the evil spirit answered and said, Jesus I know, and Paul I know; but who are ye?" The devil and his angels can see Jesus inside of you. (Acts 19:16) "And the man in whom the evil spirit was leaped on them, and overcame them, and prevailed against them, so that they fled out of that house naked and wounded."

We have no power of our own to bind demons. Gifts are spiritually discerned by God's anointed. Yes priests, pastors, and teachers make the mistake of trying to discern on their own. As you read in Acts the 19th chapter trying to use a gift you do not have can be costly. We will talk more about that later.

Let's get back to these gifts that reveal your talents. Once you know your talents the revelation of your assignment will begin to unfold before your eyes. Your assignment will lead you to your destiny. Your destiny is your purpose in life. It is the very existence of you being here.

After all no man can discern the needs of the congregation wants, do's and don'ts. The Lord himself preaches through us. The Holy Ghost is the discerner of his people. That's the power on the inside directing you to your destiny. Complete your assignment by fulfilling your destiny. You will not know who you are in the fullness until you come to Jesus. Read 1st Corinthians chapter 12 verses 1-31.

Remember every one of us is born with gifts. Who we submit ourselves to is what determines whether or not these gifts are developed properly or not. (John 10:1) "Verily, verily, I say unto you, He that entereth not by the door into the sheepfold, but climbeth up some other way, the same is a thief and a robber." You cannot go around him and it is certain you cannot run from him. It is a waste of energy and time. Let us not forget what happened to Jonah in the Old Testament. Run towards Jesus and find out your assignment. Every one of us has an assignment that we were given to work with our gifts. Jonah came to his senses after the Lord put him in the belly of a whale. What is it going to take for you to come to your senses? When you attempt to run from the Lord it's not just your life being affected. Your family and ones assigned to you are all affected. Please keep these scriptures in your mind. (Hosea 4:6) "My people are destroyed for lack of knowledge: because thou hast rejected knowledge, I will also reject thee, that thou shalt be no priest to me: seeing thou hast forgotten the law of thy God, I will also forget thy children." (Jeremiah 1:4-5) "Then the word of the Lord came unto me, saying, Before I formed thee in the belly I knew thee; and before thou camest forth out of the womb I sanctified thee, and I ordained thee a prophet unto the nations." As you continue reading in this chapter you will see that the Lord doesn't care about your age. Be ye obedient to his word. A prophet is a preacher and a preacher is a messenger of God.

Nobody has the right to keep you from your divine assignment. Please do not let them. Always remember (1 John 4:4) "Ye are of God, little children, and have overcome them: because greater is he that is in you, than he that is in the world."

You are responsible for your own soul salvation. You matter to Jesus and to those who you are assigned to woman of God.

Chapter 6

Laborers of the Gospel

L et us look in the Bible staying in the King James Version and focusing on the female laborers of the gospel. Some have chosen to ignore these scriptures but the word said in the book of: (Revelation 22:19) "And if any man shall take away from the words of the book of this prophecy, God shall take away his part out of the book of life, and out of the holy city, and from the things which are written in this book."

The laborers were in groups of two or more depending on their assignment. For instance if you look in the book of Acts of the Apostles they were in groups. (Acts 1:13) "And when they were come in, they went up into an upper room, where abode both Peter, and James, and John, and Andrew, Philip, and Thomas, Bartholomew, and Matthew, James the son of Alphaeus, and Simon Zelotes, and Judas the brother of James." (Acts 1:14) "These all continued with one accord in prayer and supplication, with the women, and Mary the mother of Jesus, and with his brethren."

The only job a laborer has is to feed the people the word of God. The method by which an individual laborer chooses to feed the people is determined by the gifts of God. For instance in the book of: (Judges 4:4) "And Deborah, a prophetess, the wife of Lapidoth, she judged Israel at that time."(Judges 4:5) "And she dwelt under the palm tree of Deborah between Ramah and Bethel in mount Ephraim: and the children of Israel came up to her for judgment." Let me ask you a question, was there a difference in what she did and what Moses did with the Israelites? Search the scriptures you may be surprised at what you may find. Deborah, a woman preacher who heard the word of the Lord directly; had multiple gifts and was not afraid to use them.

To judge God's people you must have wisdom, knowledge and understanding. Most of all you cannot have any respect of persons. If Jesus has not equipped you with these gifts you cannot be an effective leader. The most effective leader is one who is led by the spirit. He or she has only one boss and his name is Jesus the almighty God. Don't take my word for it read the book of Judges for your self. It goes on further showing the demonstration of the Holy Spirit. (Matthew 9:36) "But when he saw the multitudes, he was moved with compassion on them, because they fainted, and were scattered abroad, as sheep having no shepherd." (Matthew 9:37) "Then saith he unto his disciples, The harvest truly is plenteous, but the labourers are few; "(Matthew 9:38) "Pray ye therefore the Lord of harvest, that he will send forth labourers into his harvest."

One of the many reasons why the laborers are so few is not enough praying is being done from the pulpit to the door. From the eldest to the youngest prayer must be done on a regular basis. Can you imagine what the world would be like if every household would pray?

When you pray you begin to see with spiritual eyes and hear what thus sayest the Lord. (Joel 2:28) "And it shall come to pass afterward, that I will pour out my spirit upon all flesh; and your sons and your daughters shall prophesy, your old men shall dream dreams, your young men shall see visions:" (Joel 2:29) "And also upon the servants and upon the handmaids in those days will I pour out my spirit."

When the spirit man is in charge you are apt to make lesser mistakes. That is not to say we will be perfect, because there is only one who is perfect; our Lord Jesus Christ. (Colossians 1:28) "Whom we preach, warning every man, and teaching every man in all wisdom; that we may present every man perfect in Christ Jesus:"

One might infer that we women are not to be perfect therefore we are all right just like we are. We all know that all of us were born in sin and are far from perfect. Our God is always perfect, and he is our Saviour the Lord Jesus Christ who was led as a lamb to be slaughtered. He had no sins but bore our sins upon that body of flesh. (Isaiah 53:5) "But he was wounded for our transgressions, he was bruised for our iniquities: the chastisement of our peace was upon him; and with his stripes we are healed." That is the Old Testament evidence of truth. Now lets see what the New Testament evidence said in : (John 1:29) "The next day John seeth Jesus coming unto him, and saith, Behold the Lamb of God, which taketh away the sin of the world." Do you know any man or woman that can take away your sins? Do not answer that question we will come back to that question at a later time.

Come with me to the book of Philippians the fourth chapter and let us read about the laborers who just happen to be females. (Philippians 4:3) "And I intreat thee also, true yokefellow, help those women which laboured with me in the gospel, with Clement also, and with other my fellowlabourers, whose names are in the book of life." Now if you recall this is Paul speaking to the church. The only labor in the gospel is feeding the people by preaching and teaching the word. Your soul must be fed by the word daily for the spirit man to survive.

It takes a preacher with the mantle of God upon him or her to unlock the hidden word in your heart. Once the word is unlocked the mystery of the revelation is revealed. Please read the 3rd chapter of Ephesians verses 1-21 it is our blessing. Are you ready to be blessed woman of God? "Hold fast to the word and be not faithless" sayest the Lord.

Surely you know a preacher cannot be silent. (1st Corinthians 14:34) "Let your women keep silence in the churches: for it is not permitted unto them to speak; but they are commanded to be under obedience, as also saith the law." That would be a contradiction to his word. (1st Corinthians 14:33) "For God is not the author of confusion, but of peace, as in all churches of the saints." The women were preaching and teaching the gospel of Jesus Christ right alongside of the men. (2nd Corinthians 3:17) "Now the Lord is that Spirit: and where the Spirit of the Lord is, there is liberty." Freedom for all who seek to do his will.

Faith unlocks the door to infinite possibilities for any believer male or female. If you doubt the word read on further in the book of Romans. (Romans 16:1-2) "I COMMEND unto you Phebe our sister, which is a servant of the church which is at Cenchrea: That ye receive her in the Lord, as becometh saints, and that ye assist her in whatsoever business she hath need of you: for she hath been a succourer of many, and of myself also." Now remember this is Paul speaking here unto the people. Please notice how he encouraged the preachers to work together and assist Phebe a servant of the church. All preachers are servants of our Lord Jesus. Their job is to feed the people with the word in every circumstance. The word succor means "to go to the aid of" in the 11th edition of the Merriam-Webster Collegiate Dictionary. In other words it means rendering assistance to someone in distress. Here was another woman of God being commended by Paul for helping many preachers including himself while they were in distress.

Preaching the gospel was not an easy task back then or now. One has to give honor where honor is due. (Romans 16:3) "Greet Priscilla and Aquila my helpers in Christ Jesus:" (Romans 16:4) "Who have for my life laid down their own necks: unto whom not only I give thanks, but also all the churches of the Gentiles." (Romans 16:5) "Likewise greet the church that is in their house. Salute my wellbeloved Epaenetus, who is the firstfruits of Achaia unto Christ." In case you did not know Priscilla and Aquila were a husband and wife ministry team. Yes they both were preachers who did not mind sticking out their own necks for others as Paul states in verse 4 of the 16th chapter of Romans.

Not to change the subject, but they had a church in their house. A real preacher sent by God will feed the people the word of God anywhere he sends them. Why because Jesus is a God of no respect of persons. Your color, creed, sex, nor nationality, do not matter. All he wants is a willing vessel that will give him free course in their mind, body and soul. Let us look back in Romans on further at the 6th verse of that same chapter.

(Romans 16:6) "Greet Mary, who bestowed much labour on us." Preachers have to preach to one another. We must encourage one another through the word and through prayer and fasting. Thank God for the male and female helpers of the gospel.

Chapter 7

The Living Temple

The living temple is neither male nor female. It is a vessel of honor or dishonor. It all depends on what you have been feeding your soul which is the temple of the Lord Jesus Christ. Our bodies are vessels of the Lord Jesus which carry a soul. That soul must eat good food just like that natural body. Have you heard that saying we are what we eat? It is a true saying we are what we eat spiritually and naturally. We must be very careful when it comes to eating spiritually and naturally. Everything we eat is not good for us and some things can harm us in more ways than one. In order to protect the living temple you will need teaching on a regular basis from the master himself our Lord Jesus Christ.

Feed your soul more than your body because the body cannot live without the soul. It is the soul that keeps you alive and out of danger because of our Lord Jesus who made us.

(Psalms 37:23) "The steps of a good man are ordered by the Lord: and he delighteth in his way." Let us get understanding of this verse. Is it saying only the steps of a man are good and therefore are ordered by the Lord? Where does that leave the women? This just goes to show you what he said for one he said to the other. Male and female are alike in Jesus. Is that not what it saids in the scripture? (Galatians 3:28) "There is neither Jew nor Greek, there is neither bond nor free, there is neither male nor female: for ye are all one in Christ Jesus." (Galatians 3:29) "And if ye be Christ's, then are ye Abraham's seed, and heirs according to the promise."

All our Lord Jesus needs is a willing mind to do his will. When the mind is willing the heart and body will follow accordingly. (1st Corinthians 3:16) "Know ye not that ye are the temple of God, and that the Spirit of God dwelleth in you?" (1st Corinthians 3:17) "If any man defile the temple of God, him shall God destroy; for the temple of God is holy, which temple ye are." The ministry comes out of the spirit of the living God not out of the flesh. It is a gift from God our Lord and Saviour Jesus Christ.

The flesh is an enemy to the spirit. It tries to rule over the spirit and causes pain and hurt. Destruction of the mind, body and soul will eventually follow. Why, because that is its ultimate goal. Do not allow the flesh to rule over the mind, body, and soul. Always remember the spirit is greater than the flesh. It must be fed and nurtured by the word to grow and increase in power that's how we keep our temple holy. How else does one expect to survive the raging storm surrounding them? (Romans 8:6) "For to be carnally minded is death; but to be spiritually minded is life and peace." (Romans 8:7) "Because the carnal mind is enmity against God: for it is not subject to the law of God, neither indeed can be." (Romans 8:8) "So then they that are in the flesh cannot please God." Whichever one you feed the most will be the one with all the power. Feed your spirit man everyday, every minute and every hour. You will live longer. Remember an idle mind is the devil's workshop. Do not let your mind be idle.

How can the women be silent? What about the spirit that is inside of them? How are you going to silence him? No man has that kind of power to silence our Lord Jesus. The fact of the matter is we do not have that kind of authority. You cannot tell Jesus to be silent in his own temple. He created us for his glory.

When he went into the temple he did what he had to do. He preached and taught the word. In other words if you are not preaching the gospel come out of the pulpit. Some of you men have no business in the pulpit. And yes some of you women have no business being in the pulpit. Why, because your flesh is out of control. Laborers of the Gospel must be in control of their flesh. Keep your temple holy and the flesh will not rule.

One should be able to identify a man of God or a woman of God by the words that they speak. The outward appearance is deceitful. They look saintly on the outside but the Bible declares that their heart is like raven wolves. (Matthew 7:15) "Beware of false prophets, which come to you in sheep's clothing, but inwardly they are ravening wolves." As a matter of fact they will fool the very elect. How do I know this? because it is written in the Holy Bible; our book of truth. (Matthew 24:24) "For there shall arise false Christs, and false prophets, and shall shew great signs and wonders; insomuch that, if it were possible, they shall deceive the very elect." Jesus is the only one who can discern the sheep from the wolf. He is the one that dwells in your temple identifying who belongs to him. Listen to your spirit man and do not be deceived.

Again I say the Lord Jesus has no respect of persons. His word does not return unto him void it shall accomplish what he sent it out to do. A man or woman who has surrendered their heart, mind, body and soul unto Jesus, are the living temples. His spirit will not dwell in an unclean temple. A living temple worships the Lord Jesus everyday.

(2nd Corinthians 6:16) "And what agreement hath the temple of God with idols? for ye are the temple of the living God; as God hath said, I will dwell in them, and walk in them; and I will be their God, and they shall be my people." (2nd Corinthians 6:17) "Wherefore come out from among them, and be ye separate, saith the Lord, and touch not the unclean thing; and I will receive you," (2nd Corinthians 6:18) "And will be a Father unto you, and ye shall be my sons and daughters, saith the Lord Almighty."

What it all comes down to, is this, are you living a holy life or not? Because, when you are living holy nothing comes before Jesus. You will learn to put him first in every thing and watch your self grow in the spirit.

The living temple is fed by praying, fasting and reading God's word. Everything we need to nourish the spirit man is contained in the Holy Bible from Genesis to Revelation. All is required is a willing mind to read the words found in the Holy Bible.

Are you a living temple? Yes or no? If you are these characteristics should be found on the inside working on the outside. All of the fruits of the spirit found in Galatians the 5th chapter. (Galatians 5:22) "But the fruit of the Spirit is love, joy, peace, longsuffering, gentleness, goodness, faith," (Galatians 5:23) "Meekness, temperance: against such there is no law." Every living temple must have and display these traits at all times. Two more very important traits would be an obedient spirit and a repenting heart.

No one should have to guess at who you are. They should know without a shadow of a doubt who; you represent. They should be able to see, hear, and feel Jesus when you are around them. Angels are preachers in disguise. (Hebrews 13:2) "Be not forgetful to entertain strangers: for thereby some have entertained angels unawares." As a matter of fact be careful for nothing.

Chapter 8

Preacher Speak the Truth

Jesus our Lord and Saviour said his word shall not return unto him void. If we will not praise him he will cause the rocks to praise him in our place. Come what may he will get his glory. The same goes for preaching, whether you are male or female. Whosoever is a willing vessel that possesses the characteristics of a living temple as we discussed in the previous chapter, must obey him.

Some vessels like animals and rocks have no soul, but yet Jesus can make them do whatever he commands. How do we know this? Turn with me to the book of Numbers and read chapter 22 verses 21-35. It's right there in black and white just as plain as can be.

I do not know any talking donkeys do you? That just goes to show you his omnipotent power. If the preacher will not speak up for that which is right he will cause somebody else to take his/her place. A real preacher is bought with a price and totally sold out for Jesus. (1st Corinthians 7:23) "Ye are bought with a price; be not ye the servants of men." For Jesus I live and for Jesus I die is a real preacher's attitude. The Lord does not need any coward soldiers. Fear is a natural response but fear him who holds the power over life and death in the palm of his hand. Look back in the book of Judges the 7th chapter verses 1-25 and see what our Lord told Gideon. Don't just take my word for it. Our God is very wise, we need to listen and follow his instructions completely because deliverance is in our obedience.

Some pastors have asked our Lord Jesus to send them help and because the help was not in the vessel they wanted (male) they rejected the help. They should ask themselves who have they really rejected? If the Lord Jesus can speak through a Jackass surely he can speak through a woman. I know for a fact we are a more worthy vessel than an animal because they have no soul. After all we were created in his image to give him praise. (Genesis 1:27) "So God created man in his own image, in the image of God created he him; male and female created he them."

Our Lord Jesus is looking for some bold soldiers to preach his gospel. When I was in the world and had something to say I did not hesitate. Most of all I was not afraid to speak my mind. Every now and then Jesus reminds me of what he put on the inside. (I John 4:4) "Ye are of God, little children, and have overcome them: because greater is he that is in you, than he that is in the world." Before you say he was talking to children I am an adult. May I also remind you, all of us are God's children, saved and un-saved.

Some of the so called Church folks are in for a rude awakening come Judgement Day. Why? Because some of them had the audacity to presume to tell God's people who can preach and who cannot.

Boldness is a positive attribute when used correctly to build-up character. However it can be used as a tool of the devil to tear down character against those who appear to be weakminded. That's why

Jesus gave us his word to strengthen and empower our minds, bodies and souls. Please look at the following verses: (Matthew 11:28-30) "Come unto me, all ye that labour and are heavy laden, and I will give you rest. Take my yoke upon you, and learn of me; for I am meek and lowly in heart: and ye shall find rest unto your souls. For my yoke is easy, and my burden is light."

Our Lord Jesus has taken away any excuse we can think of for not being obedient to him. Surrender everything unto him. One might ask, what do I mean by that? You must surrender your heart, mind, body and soul. The burdens you carry give them to Jesus. You cannot rest peaceably until you do.

His yoke is the word from Genesis to Revelation. Read it, digest it and most of all believe every word. That's what a real preacher would do in any given situation. How else would you know whose for you and whose against you? Everyone that grins in your face is not for you, and yes suffice it to say that includes family. Some of your worst enemies will be family. Why because they believe they know who you are. Remember that old expression I knew you when you were . . . The key word being were.

Your past does not matter to the Lord. All your sins have been forgotten and most of all forgiven. Jesus has given you a clean slate. What are you doing with your life?

You see when you move self, family and all other carnalities out of the way, and allow Jesus to take over; some miraculous things can happen. (Ephesians 6:10) "Finally, my brethren, be strong in the Lord, and in the power of his might." (Ephesians 6:11) "Put on the whole armour of God, that ye may be able to stand against the wiles of the devil." (Ephesians 6:12) "For we wrestle not against flesh and flood, but against principalities, against powers, against the rulers of the darkness of this world, against spiritual wickedness in high places."

Male or female God's word is true. Read that entire chapter to really grasp what Jesus is saying. The real preacher must stand and speak with holy boldness. They will not take down for the devil. They will not be afraid to speak what thus saith the Lord. (Jeremiah 1:8) "Be not afraid of their faces: for I am with thee to deliver thee, saith the Lord." He will deliver us if we are obedient and do what he says. We have nothing to fear, nothing.

All Jesus is looking for is some holy vessels willing to preach his gospel in season and out of season. No one and nothing will stop them or get in their way. They will not compromise his doctrine. They will deliver the word without fear of retaliation as Jesus gives it to them.

Will you stand up for the gospel of Jesus Christ or will you be found waiting in the balance? Choose for your self today the road less traveled. (Matthew 7:13) "Enter ye in at the strait gate: for wide is the gate, and broad is the way, that leadeth to destruction, and many there be which go in thereat:" (Matthew 7:14) "Because strait is the gate, and narrow is the way, which leadeth unto life, and few there be that find it."

In other words, just because there is a crowd it doesn't mean it's the right road or path to follow. Always follow Jesus in every aspect of your life.

Chapter 9

Who is Teaching You?

Two of my most favorite Bible verses are in the 3rd chapter of the book of Proverbs. (Proverbs 3:5) "Trust in the Lord with all thine heart; and lean not unto thine own understanding." (Proverbs 3:6) "In all thy ways acknowledge him, and he shall direct thy paths." These two Bible verses sum up what every believer must do on a daily basis after receiving the Holy Ghost.

For instance our greatest teacher was and still is our God the Lord Jesus Christ. When our Lord Jesus came to earth did he not preach and teach everywhere he went? His disciples were taught to watch and pray in the spirit. (Leviticus 19:18) "Thou shalt not avenge, nor bear any grudge against the children of thy people, but thou shalt love thy neighbor as thyself: I am the Lord."

One might say what does this have to do with women preaching and teaching the gospel? Follow me in the word to St. John the 20th chapter. Who was the first person at the sepulchre?

Oh yes that would be Mary Magdalene who just happens to be a woman. That was not the same woman who anointed him for his burial? In those days it was the custom to wash your guest's feet when you entered a home; which the men didn't bother to do that either.

Now according to 1ˢᵗ Timothy chapter 3 verses 11and 12 and 1ˢᵗ Corinthians chapter 14:34-35 women are to be silent and ask questions only of their husbands. Please explain to me why Jesus our God appeared to her at the tomb alone and gave her a message. (John 20:16) "Jesus saith unto her, Mary. She turned herself, and saith unto him, Rabboni; which is to say, Master." Please remember no one can call you master because he alone is master of the universe. As a matter of fact he alone is God. (John 20:17) "Jesus saith unto her, Touch me not; for I am not yet ascended to my Father: but go to my brethren, and say unto them, I ascend unto my Father, and your Father; and to my God, and your God." (John 20:18) "Mary Magdalene came and told the disciples that she had seen the Lord, and that he had spoken these things unto her." Jesus considered her a worthy vessel and he is God. The servant is not greater than the master, what other explanation is there? (John 20:19) "Then the same day at evening, being the first day of the week, when the doors were shut where the disciples were assembled for fear of the Jews, came Jesus and stood in the midst, and saith unto them, Peace be unto you."

The Spirit walked through the walls which is our father who created us. The son which is the body of flesh revealed the wounds and the scars. (John 20:25) "The other disciples therefore said unto him, We have seen the Lord. But he said unto them, Except I shall see in his hands the print of the nails, and put my finger into the print of the nails, and thrust my hand into his side, I will not believe." (John 20:26) "And after eight days again his disciples were within, and Thomas with them: then came Jesus, the doors being shut, and stood in the midst, and said, Peace be unto you." (John 20:27) "Then saith he to Thomas, Reach hither thy finger, and behold my hands; and reach hither thy hand, and thrust it into my side: and be not faithless, but believing." Jesus is speaking here. (John 20:28) "And Thomas answered and said unto him, My Lord and my God." (John 20:29) "Jesus saith unto him, Thomas, because thou hast seen me, thou hast believed: blessed are they that have not seen, and yet have believed." There is no way that Jesus could have known what Thomas had said; except he be our God. Jesus is God manifested in the flesh to redeem us from our sins. Please do not deny his word.

The disciples were hiding while the women were looking for Jesus. They believed his word that he would rise again. The Holy Ghost is the power on the inside "reconciling the world back unto himself." Yes Jesus is Father in creation, he created the world and you and me. Please see Genesis 1:1 and read Isaiah 53:5 Jesus is son as redeemer; "with his stripes we are healed." And Holy Ghost power on the inside with the evidence of speaking in tongues as he gives us utterance. Suffice it to say there is only one true teacher our Lord and Saviour Jesus Christ. When you have received him on the inside the teacher is always present. (Proverbs 18:21) "Death and life are in the power of the tongue: and they that love it shall eat the fruit thereof." When you choose Jesus as your Saviour you have chosen life. The more time you spend with him the more he will teach you. The power on the inside will begin to manifest itself on the outside. You will speak what you hear your Father on the inside speaking. The Father is the spirit who empowers us to fulfill our destiny. Remember your destiny is your purpose in life.

If "I AM" is not inside of you teaching than who is? "I AM is your God whose name is Jesus. Read chapter 2 of the book of 1st Corinthians for further clarification.

You must understand the word of the Lord for yourself. There are people assigned to you to help and some to destroy. That's why you need the Holy Spirit on the inside discerning who is foe and who is friend. Common sense would tell you that the Lord Jesus does not contradict himself. After all God is not the author of confusion and neither can he tell a lie. Search the scriptures his word is truth from Genesis to Revelation.

Deborah did not usurp authority over the men. She stood up and spoke what Jesus put in her mouth and judged accordingly. She did not do anything wrong, and neither are you woman of God. Who empowered Deborah to speak? No one but Jesus our God gave her the wisdom, knowledge and understanding.

Did you read about the Elect Lady Lydia in (Acts 16:14) "And a certain woman named Lydia, a seller of purple, of the City of Thyatira, which worshiped God, heard us: whose heart the Lord opened, that she attended unto the things which were spoken of Paul." Not only did she obey the spirit but look at what happened in the next verse. (Acts16:15) "And when she was baptized, and her household, she besought us, saying, If ye have judged me to be faithful to the Lord, come into my house, and abide there. And she constrained us." Her entire household and generations to come was saved because of her obedience. Please always remember obedience is better than sacrifice.

We are responsible for all of our actions good and bad. Our Lord and King Jesus put more than life inside of us. We are works in progress; only he who started the work can finish the work. He alone is God. We ought to teach good things so that our children and the generations to come grow up teaching the same things.

Every child of the King is assigned a people. We must stir up that which is inside of us and awaken the gifts of our destiny. In the scriptures it is written (Psalm 42:7) "Deep calleth unto deep at the noise of thy waterspouts: all thy waves and thy billows are gone over me."

The ones we are assigned to will be drawn to us by the spirit. He will teach us all things. He who? The answer to that question is your God. Whosoever teaches you is assigned to you. What they teach you, will reveal who assigned them.

For instance I had been in church all my life, but the church wasn't completely in me. I was taught all about the scriptures, but very little on the spirit. But one day my whole life changed because I asked the Lord to bring me closer to him and bless me with a saved husband. I am a witness that Jesus answers prayers. I met a young man who was filled with the Holy Ghost and preached and sang like no other I had ever heard. I described his voice as the sing song voice because I did not know anything about the anointing at that time. I remember asking my Dad why the other preachers didn't have the sing song voice. He told me "everyone has different gifts."

My husband took me to meet his teacher the late Bishop M. Alleyne. Yes she was a woman of God who did not mind praising the Lord. A woman like no other I have ever met. When you were around her you could feel the presence of the Lord. It was a feeling of unconditional love that surpasses all understanding and made every thing better.

The spirit of the living God would preach through her non-stop. I had never seen or heard anyone preach or teach from sun up to sun down without a break. What Jesus put in her no man can take away. To this day I have not met or heard any preacher like her. Because of this woman's obedience I received in one decade what some people learn in a life time; the revelation of Jesus Christ without compromise. The mantle of the living God our Lord Jesus Christ is upon me now more than ever to reveal the mystery unto his people.

Again I ask this question who is teaching you? Paul came across many people in his journey to Macedonia. Another woman in particular he spoke about in (Acts 16:1) "Then came he to Derbe and Lystra: and, behold, a certain disciple was there, named Timotheus, the son of a certain woman, which was a Jewess, and believed; but his father was a Greek:" (Acts 16:2)

"Which was well reported of by the brethren that were at Lystra and Iconium." (Acts 16:3) "Him would Paul have to go forth with him; and took and circumcised him because of the Jews which were in those quarters: for they knew all that his father was a Greek." (Acts 16:4) "And as they went through the cities, they delivered them the decrees for to keep, that were ordained of the apostles and elders which were at Jerusalem." (Acts 16:5) "And so were the churches established in the faith, and increased in number daily." Why because a woman believed God's servants and obeyed the law. She went down in the water in Jesus name and her family followed suit. Wonderful things happen when we obey the Lord Jesus Christ.

Chapter 10

Courageous Acts of Women

From the beginning of time Jesus has had women doing great things that have saved nations. Women are givers and give 100% in various ways.

When Mary was told she would have a son did she submit herself to the Lord? Yes. Jesus chose her to be the vessel through which he came in the flesh. She knew it was her destiny. The spirit man inside of her accepted the assignment that she was born to do. The spirit man is God's spirit inside of us as you may recall from chapter 5. The angel Gabriel was a witness to what the spirit had already revealed to her (who he was). Mary fulfilled her purpose. Are you fulfilling your purpose woman of God?

Salvation did not come to us until Jesus our God came in the flesh through a virgin named Mary. Read the book of Luke 1:26-30 it's all right there in black and white. In the book of (Acts 4:12) "Neither is there salvation in any other: for there is none other name under heaven given among men, whereby we must be saved." The name of Jesus is the only name that can save you. Read these verses for yourself Isaiah 9:6 and Matthew 1:23.

Another example we find women doing courageous things is in the book of Joshua. Do you recall the story of the woman Rahab and how she hid the men of God. (James 2:25) "Likewise also was not Rahab the harlot justified by works, when she had received the messengers, and had sent them out another way?" Who hid them? A woman who was known for her reputation as being an harlot. Jesus is showing us he can use anybody who allows him. Saved or unsaved and as we already know from our previous reading in chapter 8, animals too.

Rahab chose to protect God's people because somewhere in the back of her mind she had been taught about the Lord. Again the spirit man brought what she had been taught back to her remembrance. She risked her life to save Joshua's spies from detection. The reward she received was greater than the risk. When you give your life to Jesus he will save it. (Matthew 10:39) "He that findeth his life shall lose it: and he that loseth his life for my sake shall find it." In this case Rahab saved her entire family physically and spiritually from generations to come. Why, because each person is responsible for another generation. When one runs the gene pool you will see that the loins of Christ came down through Abraham. Read in the book of Matthew and follow the genealogy. (Matthew 1:1) "The book of the generation of Jesus Christ, the son of David, the son of Abraham." The whole chapter starts from the beginning listing the generations in order.

Another courageous woman who stands out in the Bible was Esther. She was a queen but in those days the custom of those times did not allow her to speak to the king. Yes he was her husband but even she could not ask him questions until she was summoned to the inner court. Esther was queen to the king but a servant to Jesus our God. (Esther 3:8) "And Haman said unto king Ahasuerus, There is a certain people scattered abroad and dispersed among the people in all the provinces of thy kingdom; and their laws are diverse from all people; neither keep they the king's laws: therefore it is not for the king's profit to suffer them."(Esther 3:9) "If it please the king, let it be written that they may be destroyed: and I will pay ten thousand talents of silver to the hands of those that have the charge of the business, to bring it into the king's treasuries." When she was made aware of the situation she too risked her life and spoke to the king unannounced. The penalty for coming or going into the inner court without being called was death. Her obedience saved her life, her people and countless others. She is a perfect example of being not afraid of their faces. Fear makes you react without thinking. Queen Esther did not panic because she knew the battle was not hers. The battle belongs to the Lord Jesus and he alone will fight for you. Always remember the battle belongs to the Lord. It is not your fight.

The spirit is always greater than the flesh. Jesus gives you peace in the midst of the storm. There is a end to every storm and the time is now sayest the Lord.

Queen Esther knew the word that this too goest out by fasting and praying. Her people had to fast and pray along with her while she implemented her plan of action. This plan of action could have only come from Jesus. Remember what it said in the scripture (Matthew 10:19) "But when they deliver you up, take no thought how or what ye shall speak: for it shall be given you in that same hour what ye shall speak."

He will give you exactly what you need when the time comes. Please read the book of Esther her plan was flawless. Queen Esther received favor and deliverance beyond her wildest imagination and the enemy was defeated. Glory hallelujah! Jesus came through for Queen Esther and her people. Our God the Lord Jesus Christ taught her and her people what to do and delivered them for their obedience. I am sure there are many more courageous women in the Bible working behind the scenes.

If you require further proof please read 2nd Kings the 22nd chapter and the 23rd chapter because both offer some more interesting reading on how our God the Lord Jesus uses women mightily. Here we have a high priest named Hilkiah, Shaphan the scribe, his son Ahikam, and Achbor, and a servant named Asahiah ordered by the King to obtain word from the Lord. These men were ordered by King Josiah to obtain word from Huldah the prophetess. Please pay special attention to this verse. (2nd Kings 22:14) "So Hilkiah the priest, and Ahikam, and Achbor, and Shaphan, and Asahiah, went unto Huldah the prophetess, the wife of Shallum the son of Tikvah, the son of Harhas, keeper of the wardrobe; (now she dwelt in Jerusalem in the college;) and they communed with her." They had to seek her for the word of the Lord was in her and it was not an easy word that she had for them.

Be not afraid to speak what thus sayest the Lord." I am with thee. I am your God." Jesus is speaking unto his people hear ye him." I will speak in whom so ever will let me male or female."

Do we have any courageous women out there willing to work for Jesus? Imagine how many lives would be saved. One person can make a difference all you have to do is believe.

Conclusion

What is it going to take for you to be taught? Better yet is the right one teaching you? Check their qualifications out thoroughly using the scriptures.

Everyone has a message to deliver but the spirit man has to reveal to you the method to release it. The message is for the ones whom you have been assigned to and will only be received by them. Heard the saying the teacher is always present when the student is ready to learn? Let me let you in on a secret, we are always students in God's eyes.

The spirit man is waiting to unlock the greatness in you woman of God. For the word says in (1 John 4:4) "Ye are of God, little children, and have overcome them: because greater is he that is in you, than he that is in the world." It also said in the word the servant is not greater than the master. The master is Jesus the almighty God. Are you greater than the master man of God? Whether you believe this word or not it is your prerogative. However please know this, nothing that is written in this book is without sufficient proof from the Holy Bible. Only a foolish person would argue against the word of God. Jesus said he will move a stumbling block which is anything or anybody that tries to hinder the word of God from going forth to his people. Let us all walk in holiness and truth for we are all one in Christ Jesus.

Woman you were created for God's glory to help the man spread the gospel. If you do not do what Jesus has called you to do, the blood will be required at your hands. (Ezekiel 3:18) "When I say unto the wicked, Thou shalt surely die; and thou givest him not warning, nor speakest to warn the wicked from his wicked way, to save his life; the same wicked man shall die in his iniquity; but his blood will I require at thine hand." You will not escape the calling on your life no matter where you go. Jesus is every where and he will not take any excuses, speak on the pulpit, the floor, or the streets until the Lord calls you home.

Equality belongs to everyone and it is about time God's people realize this. Everyone needs to take their rightful place that has been ordained before the foundation of the world. Yes I know that there are some people who believe that a woman's body is too fragile to preach the gospel. Apparently they never heard the word in (Jeremiah 32:27) "Behold, I am the Lord, the God of all flesh: is there anything too hard for me?"

Please remember that there are other people affected by every decision you make. Think about your children. Jesus said in (Hosea 4:6) "My people are destroyed for lack of knowledge: because thou has rejected knowledge, I will also reject thee, that thou shalt be no priest to me: seeing thou hast forgotten the law of thy God, I will also forget thy children." Our Lord Jesus is not playing with any of us he means exactly what he says. If you forget about him he will forget about your children. If our generation won't adhere to the word who will? Let us be good examples worthy of God's grace. Holy vessels preaching and teaching every where we go. Surrender to the mantle of God that is on your life and be not led astray by false doctrine. Just say here I am Lord please show me my assignment, for it is my desire to please you and you alone, because you alone are God.

Jesus is God and he created us male and female a like. (Genesis 1:27) "So God created man in his own image, in the image of God created he him; male and female created he them." In Jesus Name speak what thus sayest the Lord God of Israel!

Words of Encouragement for All of God's People

STAND

In the midst of the storm I feel the wind.

It's swirling and swirling but it never ends.

I try to stand as sturdy as I can, but feel my legs going out from under me again.

Hold on I say,

Hold on, it will pass just like before.

Oh no here comes the rain.

I'm beginning to tire,

My body is reeling back and forth.

I won't survive another blow.

Help me Jesus!

Then I heard his voice.

Peace be still!

Here comes the overflow!

VICTORY

The battle is already won.

The enemy is defeated.

Our burdens uplifted.

All yokes destroyed.

Faith united into one.

Fear is abandoned.

All doubt is dismissed.

Our healing is set free.

Power is discovered.

Power is released.

All in Jesus Name!

Author Contact Information:

Elder Cheryl Chavis

P.O. BOX 13090

Greensboro, NC 27415

Phone # 1-866-763-8701

Fax # 1-866-763-8701

Customer Order Information:

Order Books at
www.Xlibris.com

Get Published, Inc!
Thorofare, NJ 08086
01 April, 2010
BA2010091